The Incredible Bible Stories

Volume 2

Selvi Piyatina

Profile

"The Incredible Bible Stories, Volume 2" is a captivating collection of ten inspiring tales from the Old Testament, all centered around the remarkable figure of Moses. The miraculous beginning of Prophet Moses, extraordinary events that demonstrated God's power in Egypt, a pivotal moment during the Exodus (the death of the firstborn), the iconic event of the parting of the Red Sea, the Ten Commandments to guide humanity, God's provision of Manna and Quail in the wilderness, a cautionary tale about rebellion Korah, the talking donkey of Balaam, teachings on wisdom and guidance by Moses, and the conclusion of Moses' work as a legacy of God.

This book is an ideal resource for children and families seeking to delve deeper into the rich narratives of the Bible. Through these stories, readers will glean valuable lessons on faith, trust, obedience, and perseverance—essential virtues for life. Parents and teachers alike will find it a valuable tool for instilling these timeless values in young hearts.

Selvi Piyatina, MBA

Dedication

This book is lovingly dedicated to my father, the late S. P. Anthony Cruze, a valiant wounded veteran of the Indian Army. His sacrifices and valour were the beacon that inspired me to chase my dreams and stand firm against adversity. He was the architect of my perseverance and the champion of hard work.

In equal measure, I dedicate this work to my mother, the late Mary Stella Cruze, a steadfast pillar of support alongside my father and my guiding star. Their unwavering faith and boundless love for me have been the wind beneath my wings, propelling me to embrace my passion.

To my parents, to whom I owe my all, this book stands as a tribute—a testament to the seeds of knowledge they sowed in my heart and the dreams they nurtured, allowing me to turn them into reality.

Acknowledgements

My deepest gratitude is extended to the Almighty for the knowledge and inspiration bestowed upon me in the writing of this book. His guidance has been indispensable.

I wish to convey my heartfelt thanks to my husband, Dr G. Rajendran, and my son, R. Jasper Sheleph, for their unwavering support and assistance throughout this journey. Special thanks are due to Pastor T. Durairaj for his invaluable supervision.

Lastly, my appreciation goes out to the readers of 'The Incredible Bible Stories, Volume 2.' Your time and support are deeply valued. It is my sincere hope that this book will not only inspire and educate but also captivate your imagination.

The Incredible Bible Stories

Volume 2

Contents

from Exodus chapter 1 to Deuteronomy chapter 34

1. PROPHET MOSES THE MAN OF GOD

The children of Israel were fruitful, increased abundantly, and multiplied, and the land of Egypt was filled with them. Then there arose a new king over Egypt, named Pharaoh, who did not know Joseph. Pharaoh said to his people that the children of Israel are more and mightier than the Egyptians. If there is a war, they will join with our enemies and fight against us. So, the Egyptians set taskmasters (*supervisors*) to afflict the people of Israel with burdens. The Egyptians made the children of Israel serve rigorously (*severity*) and made their lives bitter with harsh labour. But the more the Israelites were afflicted, the more they multiplied.

Seeing this, the King of Egypt told the Hebrew midwives Shiphrah and Puah to kill all the sons born to the Israeli women but to save the daughters. But the midwives feared God and saved the male children alive. When the King of Egypt heard about this, he called the midwives and asked, "Why have you saved the male children alive?" They said to Pharaoh, "The Hebrew women are not like the Egyptian women, but they are stronger and deliver the child before we reach their house." Since the midwives feared God, he blessed them. Then Pharaoh commanded his people to cast the male children into the river and save the females.

During this period, in the house of Levi, a woman conceived and gave birth to a son. Since the child was very good-looking, the mother hid him for three months. When she could no longer hide him, she made a basket of bulrushes (*wetland plants*), pasted it with slime (*clay having adhesive qualities*) and pitch (*sticky substance*), put the baby on it, and left it by the river's brink (*edge*). The child's sister stood far away and watched what would happen to her brother.

In the meantime, the daughter of Pharaoh came to the river to wash herself, and her maidens walked along the riverside. And Pharaoh's daughter noticed the Ark and sent her maid to fetch it. When she opened it, she saw a child, and he was weeping. She had compassion for the child and said, This is one of the Hebrew children. Noticing all these, the child's sister said to Pharaoh's daughter, Should I go and call a nurse from the Hebrew women to nurse the child? Pharaoh's daughter agreed to the same. Then the little girl went and brought her mother. Pharaoh's daughter said to the child's mother, Take the child away and nurse the baby for me, and I will pay your wages. The woman took the child and nursed him.

The woman brought the child to Pharaoh's daughter after he grew up and handed him over to her, and he became her son. She named him Moses because she drew him out of the water. When Moses was cast into the water, Pharaoh's daughter took him and nourished him as her own son. But Moses disliked being the son of Pharaoh's daughter.

Since Moses was learned and was powerful in speech and in deeds (*action*), he could possess the wisdom of the Egyptians. When he was born, he was hidden by his parents because they saw he was an angelic child, and they were not afraid of the king's commandment.

When Moses turned forty years old, he went out and visited his fellow brothers and looked at their burdens. Once, when he saw an Egyptian smiting one of his own people, he slew the Egyptian, taking up his fellow Israelite's defence, and hid him in the sand when no one noticed. The next day, when he went out, he saw two Hebrew men fighting with each other. He said to them, Why are you fighting? Then the men asked Moses, "Who made you prince and judge over us? You intend to kill us, like the way you killed the Egyptians."

Pharaoh heard this incident, and he sought to slay Moses. Having come to know that Pharaoh wanted to slay him, Moses feared for his life, fled from the face of Pharaoh, and dwelt in the land of Midian.

When Moses was sitting by the well, Reuel's (*also called Jethro, the priest of Midian*) seven daughters came to water their father's flock. When they drew water from the well and filled their troughs (*containers*), the shepherds drove them away. Seeing this, Moses helped Jethro's daughters, and he watered their flock. After they returned home, their father, Reuel, asked, "How is it that you are early today?" They said an Egyptian delivered them from the hands of the shepherds, drew enough water, and watered the flocks.

The priest asked his daughters, "Where was he, and why had they left him behind? Bring him so that he may eat bread." They brought Moses home, and he was content to dwell with the priest.

Seeing the meekness and humility of Moses, the priest gave Moses his daughter, Zipporah, to be his wife. She gave birth to a son and named him Gershom because he was a stranger in a strange land.

In the course of time, after the King of Egypt died, the children of Israel cried, and their cry reached God by reason of their bondage under the hands of the Egyptians. God heard their groaning (*suffering or sorrow*) and remembered his covenant with Abraham, Isaac, and Jacob, who had respect for them.

Moses looked after the flock of Jethro, his father-in-law. One day he led the flock to the backside of the desert and went to the mountain of God, Horeb. And the Angel of the Lord appeared to him in a flame of fire, from the midst of a bush. Moses looked at the bush, and the bush burned with fire, but it was not consumed. Moses wanted to go near the bush and see the great sight—why the bush did not burn. But when the Lord saw Moses nearing the bush, God called him out from the midst of the bush and said, Moses, Moses, and he said, "Here am I." The Lord said to Moses, "Do not come near; remove your shoes, for the place where you stand is holy ground. I am the God of thy father, the God of Abraham, the God of Isaac, and the God of Jacob." And Moses hid his face because he was afraid to look at God.

The Lord said, I have seen the affliction of my people in Egypt and have heard their cry and their sorrows because of their taskmasters. I have come down to deliver them out of the hands of the Egyptians and will bring them out of the land and take them to a large and good land flowing with milk and honey. I will send you to Pharaoh to bring the children of Israel out of Egypt. Then Moses said to God, Who am I that I should go to Pharaoh and bring the children of Israel out of Egypt? God said, I will certainly be with you, and you shall worship the Lord upon this mountain, and this shall be a token (*support for a belief*).

Moses said to God, When I go to the children of Israel and tell them that the God of your fathers has sent me, they will ask, What is his name? What shall I say to them?

God said unto Moses, You shall say, The Lord said, "I AM THAT I AM. I, the Lord God of your fathers, Abraham, Isaac, and Jacob, have sent." Therefore, go and gather the elders of Israel, and say unto them, The Lord God of your fathers has appeared and said, I have visited your affliction in Egypt and will bring you out. They will hear your voice. You shall go to the king of Egypt and say, The Lord God of the Hebrews has met us, and let us go on a three-day journey into the wilderness to offer sacrifice to the Lord our God.

"But the king of Egypt will not let you go. Then I will stretch out my hand and smite Egypt with all my wonders, after which he will let you go. When you go, you will not go empty, but every woman shall borrow her jewels of silver and gold and their garments."

Moses said they would not believe me or hear my voice. And the Lord said to him, What is in your hand? Moses said it was a rod. The Lord said, Cast it on the ground, and he cast it on the ground, and it became a serpent, and Moses fled. The Lord said to Moses, Put forth your hand and take it by the tail. Moses put his hand on it and caught it, and it became a rod in his hand. Now they will believe that the Lord God appeared to you. Further, the Lord told Moses to put his hand in his bosom (*the dress covering his chest*). Moses put his hand into his bosom and took it out; his hand was leprous as snow. The Lord told Moses to put his hand again into his bosom, and he did so. When Moses pulled his hand out, it turned normal again, just like his other flesh. If they do not believe the first sign, they will believe the second. If they do not believe both signs, then take the water of the river and pour it upon the dry land, and the water shall become blood upon the dry land.

Moses told God, I am not eloquent (*speak fluently*); I am slow of speech and tongue. Then the Lord said, "Who made man's mouth, or who made the dumb, the deaf, or the blind? Have not I, the Lord? Therefore, go, and I will be with your mouth and teach you what you shall say." Moses said, Lord, please send someone else. Hearing this, the Lord was angry with Moses and said, "Is not the Levite, your brother Aaron, there, who can speak well? He is coming to meet you, and he will be glad to see you. You will speak to Aaron and put words in his mouth, and I will be with your mouth and with his mouth, and I will teach you. Aaron shall be your spokesman to the people instead of your mouth, and you shall be to him instead of God. You shall take this rod in your hand wherever you make signs."

Moses chose to suffer affliction with the people of God rather than enjoy the pleasures of sin. He had more respect for the future rewards than for the greater riches of the treasures of Egypt. By faith, he forsook (*to give up*) Egypt without fearing the wrath (*great anger*) of the king Pharaoh and considered his as invisible.

Then Moses went to Jethro, his father-in-law, and said, Let me return to my brothers, who are in Egypt, and see if they are still alive. Jethro said to Moses, Go in peace.

The Lord said to Moses, Go to Egypt, for all the men who were after your life are dead. So he took his wife and sons, set them on an ass, and went to Egypt with the rod of God in his hand. The Lord said, After you go to Egypt, see that you do all the wonders before Pharaoh that I have put in your hands. But I will harden Pharaoh's heart so that he will not let the people go. Say to Pharaoh that the Lord says, Israel is my son and firstborn. Let my son go so that he may serve me. If you refuse, I will slay your firstborn son.

2. MOSES ROD AND MIRACLES IN EGYPT

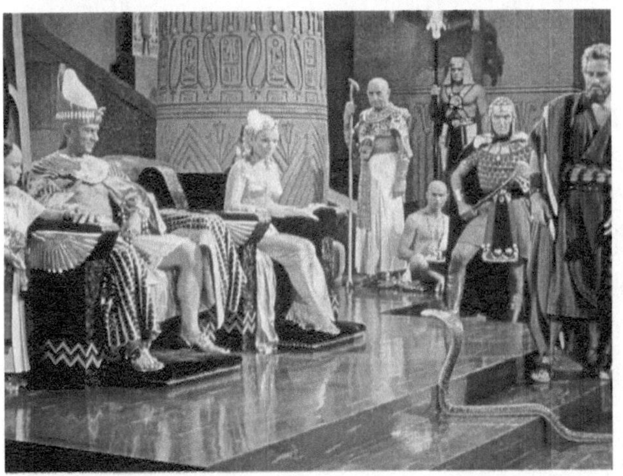

The Lord said to Aaron, "Go into the wilderness (*uncultivated, wild, or waste land*) to meet Moses, your brother." So Aaron met Moses on the mountain of God, and he kissed him. Moses told Aaron all the words of the Lord and all the signs. Then they both went and gathered all the elders of the children of Israel, and Aaron told all the words that Moses spoke to him, and he did the signs in the sight of the people. The people believed when they heard that the Lord had looked upon their affliction, and the children of Israel bowed their heads and worshipped.

Then Moses and Aaron went and told Pharaoh, the king of Egypt, that the Lord had said, "Let my people go and celebrate with a feast in the wilderness to honour me." Then Pharaoh said, Who is the Lord, that I should obey his voice and let Israel go? I neither knew the Lord nor will I let you all go. Moses and Aaron said the God of the Hebrews met with us. So we ask of you to let us go on a three-day journey into the desert and offer sacrifice to our Lord, or else pestilence (*a contagious disease*) will fall upon us.

Pharaoh told Moses and Aaron, Why are you distracting (*diverting attention*) the people from their work? And Pharaoh commanded his officers and taskmasters (*supervisors*) not to give straw to the children of Israel but to let them gather straw for themselves; however, the output of work should be the same number of bricks and not be diminished (*reduced*). So, the people were scattered throughout all of Egypt to gather stubble (*stalks left behind after harvest*) instead of straw.

The taskmasters of Egypt told the people of Israel to fulfil the work as and when straw was available. The officers of the Israelites were beaten, and they were questioned by the Egyptian taskmasters about why they had not completed their daily task of making bricks.

Then the officers of Israel went and wept before Pharaoh, saying, "We are not given straw, but are asked to make the same number of bricks and are beaten up. The fault is in your people." Then Pharaoh told them, "Since you are lazy, you keep saying that you want to go and offer sacrifice to the Lord. Go and work; no straw will be given to you, but you will have to deliver the said number of bricks daily."

The officers of the children of Israel met Moses and Aaron, who stood on the way after they were returning from Pharaoh and told them, You have made Pharaoh and his servants hate us and have put a sword in their hands to slay (*to kill*) us. Then Moses returned to the Lord and said, "Why have you treated the children of Israel so badly, and why have you sent me? I spoke to Pharaoh in your name, but Pharaoh dealt very badly with the people, and you have not delivered the people from the hands of Pharaoh."

Then the Lord said to Moses, Now you will see what I will do to Pharaoh; with a strong hand, he will drive the Israelites out of his land. I will bring you out of the burdens of Egypt and deliver you from bondage, and I will redeem (*rescue*) you. When Moses went and told the people of Israel the words of the Lord, they did not hear, for they were distressed (*emotional discomfort*).

The Lord said, Go and speak to Pharaoh, that he let the children of Israel go out of the land. Then Moses said, Lord, behold, the children of Israel have not heard me; how will Pharaoh hear me? The Lord said, "I have made you a god to Pharaoh, and Aaron, your brother, shall be your prophet. You will say all that I command you, and your brother Aaron will speak to Pharaoh. This will harden the heart of Pharaoh, and I will multiply my signs and wonders in the land of Egypt. The Egyptians shall know that I am the Lord when I bring out the children of Israel from the midst of the Egyptians." Moses and Aaron did as the Lord had commanded them.

The disastrous plagues of Egypt, from which the Lord rescued the children of Israel

Moses was eighty years old, and Aaron was eighty-three years old when all this happened. This shows that Moses life has been marked by three segments. He was 40 years old when he fled to Midian and lived in Midian for 40 years. And for the rest of his life, he followed the Lord's instructions and served the children of Israel.

The Lord said unto Moses, When Pharaoh shall say, Show a miracle, then you shall say to Aaron, Take your rod and cast it before Pharaoh, and it shall become a serpent.

Moses and Aaron went to Pharaoh, and Aaron did as the Lord had commanded, and the rod became a serpent. Then Pharaoh called the wise men and the sorcerers (*magicians*) of Egypt. The magicians of Egypt also performed in the same manner with their enchantments (*magic*). They cast down their rods, and they became serpents. But Aaron's rod swallowed up their rods. Pharaoh's heart was hardened, and he refused to let the people go.

Next, Aaron took the rod and stretched his hand upon the waters of Egypt—on streams, rivers, ponds, and pools; they turned into blood. Blood was present throughout all of Egypt, both in the vessels of wood and the vessels of stone. The fish died, the river was stinking, and the Egyptians could not drink the water. The magicians of Egypt also did so with their enchantments. But Pharaoh's heart was hardened, and he went inside his house without giving it a thought. Since they could not drink the water of the river, all the Egyptians started digging around the river for water to drink. For seven days, God had smitten the river.

Then Aaron stretched out his hand over the waters of Egypt, and the frogs came up and covered the land of Egypt. They were abundant (*plenty*) in the bedchambers of Pharaoh's and his servant's houses, in their ovens, and in their kneading troughs. Then Pharaoh called for Moses and Aaron and told them to plead to the Lord that he take away the frogs from him and from his people, and he would let the people go. Moses asked Pharaoh, When shall I pray to destroy the frogs so that they may remain in the river only? Pharaoh said tomorrow, and Moses replied, Let it be according to your word, and the frogs shall depart from you and your houses, your people, and your servants.

Moses and Aaron went out, and Moses cried to the Lord to destroy the frogs. The Lord did it according to the word of Moses. The frogs died out of the houses, villages, and fields; they were gathered into heaps, and the land stank.

When Pharaoh saw that there was a brief interval, he became stubborn and hardened his heart. Seeing this, the Lord said to Moses,

Say unto Aaron, stretch out the rod, and smite the dust of the land, so that it becomes lice throughout all the land of Egypt. They did so, and the dust turned into lice throughout Egypt. The magicians also used their enchantments to bring lice, but they could not, so there were lice upon man and beast. Then the magician told Pharaoh, This is by God. But Pharaoh's heart was hardened, and he did not listen to them.

The Lord sent a grievous swarm of flies upon Pharaoh's people, his servants, and all the houses of the Egyptians, and the land was filled with flies. God severed (*separated*) Goshen, where his people lived, and no swarm of flies affected them, and he put a division between his people and the people of Egypt.

Pharaoh then called for Moses and Aaron and said, Go, offer sacrifice to your Lord, but you should not go very far away. Moses said, I will pray to the Lord to remove the swarm of flies, but do not deceive (*cheat*) my people. The Lord did according to the word of Moses and removed the swarm of flies, but Pharaoh hardened his heart and did not let the people go.

Next, the Lord's hand was upon the cattle with grievous murrain (*an infectious disease*), where the horses, asses, camels, oxen, and sheep died. But the Lord again severed the cattle of Israel from the cattle of Egypt. All the cattle of Egypt died, but not one of the cattle of Israel died. Pharaoh's heart was hardened, and he did not let the people of Israel go.

Then, Moses took a handful of ashes from the furnace and sprinkled them towards heaven in the sight of Pharaoh. And it became little dust in all the land of Egypt and caused boils on men and beasts. The magicians could not stand before Moses because the boils were upon them and upon all Egyptians. And the Lord hardened the heart of Pharaoh.

The Lord smote the Egyptians with a hailstorm, so that they would be cut off from the earth. Moses stretched forth his hand towards heaven, which sent thunder and hail, and lightning flashed down to the ground.

Moses had instructed Pharaoh to gather their livestock and all that was in the field, or else the hail would come down upon them and they would die. Those who feared the word of the Lord among the servants of Pharaoh brought their cattle into the houses. Those who ignored the word of the Lord left their livestock and servants in the field. So there was hail, and fire mingled with hail ran along the ground upon the land of Egypt. It was the worst in all the land of Egypt since it became a nation.

The hail shattered both man and beast, every herb, breaking every tree, and all that was in the field, but in the land of Goshen, where the children of Israel lived, there was no hail. Pharaoh summoned Moses and Aaron and said to them, The Lord is righteous; my people and I are wicked; pray unto the Lord to stop the thunder and hail, and I will let you go, and you shall no longer stay.

Moses replied, As soon as I go out, I will spread my hands unto the Lord, and the thunder and hail shall cease (*to stop*), but you and your servants will still not fear the Lord God.

So Moses went out of the city and stretched his hands to the Lord; then the thunder and the hail ceased, and there was no rain.

The flax and the barley were ruined because the barley had headed and the flax was in the bud. But the wheat and rye were not ruined, for they were not grown up. When Pharaoh saw that the rain and the thunder had ceased, he sinned again. He and his servants hardened their hearts and did not let the Israelites go.

The Lord said to Moses, "I have hardened their hearts so that I can show my signs. You can tell your children and grandchildren the signs I have performed in Egypt so that they will know I am the Lord."

Moses and Aaron went to Pharaoh and said, This is what the Lord says: "How long will you refuse to send my people? If you refuse to let my people go, tomorrow I will bring locusts into your country. They will cover the face of the earth so that no one will be able to see it. They shall eat the residue that escaped from the hail, including every tree that grows in the field. They shall fill all the houses of the Egyptians, which neither your parents nor your ancestors have seen since the day they were upon the earth." After saying this, Moses went out of Pharaoh's presence.

Pharaoh's servants said to Pharaoh, How long will this man be a snare (*a mental trap*) to us? Let them go and serve their God now that Egypt is destroyed. Moses and Aaron were brought again before Pharaoh, and Pharaoh said to them, You men alone go and serve the Lord. Then Moses and Aaron were driven out of Pharaoh's presence.

The Lord said to Moses, Stretch out thine hand over the land of Egypt for the locusts, and Moses did so. The Lord caused an east wind to blow across the land all that day and night. And in the morning, the wind brought the locusts. The locusts rested on all the coasts of Egypt. They were very severe, and they covered the face of the whole earth, so that the land was darkened. They ate all the herbs and fruits of the trees, and there was nothing green on the trees or plants that the hail had left.

Then Pharaoh called for Moses and Aaron in haste and said, I have sinned against the Lord your God and against you. Therefore, forgive me this one time and pray to your God that he may take away this death from me. Moses went out and prayed to the Lord, and the Lord brought a mighty, strong west wind, which carried away the locusts and cast them into the red sea. Not one locust was left in all the territory of Egypt.

When Pharaoh's heart was hardened again, the Lord told Moses to stretch out his hand towards heaven so that there would be darkness over the land of Egypt—darkness that can be felt. Moses did so, and there was such thick darkness for three days that they were unable to see each other and did not move from their place. But the children of

Israel had light in their dwelling place. Then Pharaoh called Moses and told him, You go with your women and your little ones; let your flocks and herds stay here. But Moses said our cattle would also go with us, and not a hoof (*the human foot*) would be left behind.

Pharaoh did not let the people go, since his heart was hardened. He said to Moses, Get away from me; make sure you do not appear before me again. The day you see my face, you will die. Moses replied, You have spoken right; I will not see your face any more.

3. DEATH OF THE FIRSTBORN

God gave Pharaoh and the Egyptians several warnings, in the form of plagues, before the death of the firstborn. The Egyptians had an opportunity to repent and release the Israelites from slavery, but the Egyptians refused every time.

Even though God gave advance warning that all the firstborn sons of Egypt would die, Pharaoh still would not release the Israelites from slavery. Pharaoh and the Egyptians invited this plague upon themselves.

Finally, the Lord said to Moses, I will bring one more plague upon Pharaoh and upon Egypt. After that, he will let you leave this country, and he will surely force you out of Egypt altogether. So, speak to the Israelites and tell them that every woman borrows her jewellery of silver and gold from her neighbour.

The Lord caused the Egyptians to look favourably on the Israelites. And Moses was considered very great and respected in the sight of Pharaoh's servants and in the sight of his people.

Moses announced to Pharaoh that, "about midnight, the Lord will go out into the heart of Egypt, and all the firstborn sons shall die in every family of Egypt, from the firstborn of Pharaoh that sits upon his throne to the firstborn of the maidservants that are behind the mill, the firstborn of the captives that are in the dungeon, and all the firstborn of the beasts."

There shall be a loud cry throughout all the land of Egypt, like no one has heard before nor will hear ever again. But this will not happen to the children of Israel, and you will know how the Lord makes a difference between the Egyptians and Israelites. The Israelites will be so peaceful that even a dog will not move its tongue. Then all your Egyptian servants will come down to me and bow down, and they will beg, 'You and your people, please leave.' After that, I will go out." And he went out of sight of Pharaoh in burning anger.

The Lord said to Moses earlier, "Pharaoh will not listen to you, and I will multiply my wonders in Egypt. And Pharaoh's heart was hardened, and he would not let the Israelites leave the country."

While the Israelites were still in the land of Egypt, the Lord spoke to Moses and Aaron: "This month shall be the first month of the year; speak to the children of Israel that on the tenth day of this month, each family must choose a lamb, one lamb per household. If the family is too small to consume a whole lamb, he can share it with his next neighbour, taking into account the number of people there. Select the lamb according to the number of members and eating capacity per person."

"Choose a one-year-old male goat or lamb without any defects. You shall keep it until the fourteenth day of the month, and the whole community of Israel must slaughter them in the evening. Take a bunch of hyssops (*aromatic bushy herbs*), dip it in blood, and apply it on the two side posts and on the upper door frames of the house where you are going to eat, and none of you shall go out of your houses until morning. Roast the meat over the fire and eat it along with unleavened bread (*without using yeast*) and bitter herbs. Do not eat the meat raw or boiled in water. Do not keep the remaining until morning. If anything remains until the next morning, burn it with fire. While eating the meal, you will cover yourself, your shoes on your feet, and your rod in your hand, and eat the meal in haste. It is the Lord's Passover."

"On the same night, when I pass through the land of Egypt and see the blood on the top and sides of the door frame, I will pass over those houses, and the plague shall not destroy the firstborn, both men and beasts. But I will strike all the firstborn of men and beasts of the Egyptians, and I will execute judgement against all the gods of Egypt because I am the Lord. This day you shall remember for ever and keep a feast for the Lord throughout your generations."

Moses summoned all the elders of Israel and ordered them to do according to the instructions of the Lord. The children of Israel bowed their heads, worshipped, and followed as they were instructed.

At midnight, the Lord struck down all the firstborn in the land of Egypt, from the firstborn of Pharaoh, who sat on the throne, to the firstborn of the prisoner, who was in the dungeon, and all the firstborn of livestock as well. Pharaoh and all his servants woke up suddenly in the night, for there was a loud wailing in Egypt. There was not a house where there was not one dead.

Pharaoh called for Moses and Aaron during the night and told them, "Leave with your children, flocks, and herds, and bless me as well." The Egyptians urged the children of Israel to leave the land as quickly as possible. The Egyptians said, Otherwise, "we all will die."

The children of Israel borrowed all their jewels and garments and bound their dough before it was leavened, and the kneading troughs were bound in their clothes and carried upon their shoulders. The Egyptians lent all that the Israelites asked for. Since the Israelites were thrust out of Egypt in a great hurry, they could not prepare any food for themselves.

The children of Israel dwelt in Egypt for four hundred and thirty years (*430 years*) as hosts. At the end of four hundred and thirty years, on that very same day, all the armies of the Lord left Egypt. It was a night to be remembered for all the children of Israel in their generations. And the children of Israel journeyed by foot from Rameses to Succoth. They were about six hundred thousand men (*6,00,000*), besides women and children. Moses took the bones of Joseph with him, as Joseph took an oath from the children of Israel, "Carry my bones out of the land of Egypt."

4. PARTING OF THE RED SEA

The Lord went before the children of Israel as a pillar of cloud by day to lead them the way and a pillar of fire by night to give them light, so that they could travel by day or night. The pillar of the cloud was not removed during the day, nor the pillar of fire by night, from before the people.

The Lord said to Moses, "Journey from Succoth and encamp in Etham between Migdol and the Red Sea. Pharaoh will think, The Israelites are wandering around the land in confusion and are entangled in the desert, without an escape."

When Pharaoh and his people heard that the Israelites had fled, the Egyptians changed their minds, and their hearts were hardened. And they regretted having sent the children of Israel and said, "Why have we sent the Israelites away? We have lost their service." So, Pharaoh made ready and took six hundred (*600*) chosen chariots and all the other chariots of Egypt with captains, his horsemen, and his army, and they pursued the Israelites and overtook them while they were camping by the Red Sea.

The children of Israel noticed that Pharaoh and the Egyptians came after them, and they were terrified and cried out to the Lord. The Israelites told Moses that it would have been better for us to have served the Egyptians than to die in the wilderness. Then Moses said to the people, "Fear not; see the salvation of the Lord, which he will show you today, for you will never see the Egyptians after today. Be at peace; the Lord shall fight for you."

Then the Lord told Moses, "Why do you cry to me? Tell the children of Israel to move forward. But before that, lift up your rod and stretch out your hand over the sea to divide the water. The children of Israel shall go on dry ground through the midst of the sea. But I will harden the hearts of the Egyptians so that they will follow you."

The angel of God, who went before the camp of Israel, withdrew and went behind the Israelites, and the pillar of cloud also moved and stood behind them. The pillar of cloud was going between the Israelites and the Egyptians. It was a cloud and darkness to the Egyptians, but it gave light by night to the Israelites, and it did not allow the Egyptian armies to get closer to the Israelites.

Moses then stretched his hand over the sea, and the Lord caused the sea to go back by a strong east wind that occurred all that night and turned the sea into dry land. The water was divided and stood as a wall on either side of them, and the Israelites walked into the midst of the sea on dry ground. The

Egyptians pursued and went after the Israelites into the midst of the sea.

And the Lord looked down from the pillar of fire and cloud and troubled the Egyptian army. The Lord took off their chariot wheels so that they had difficulty driving them. The Egyptians said, "Let us flee from the face of Israel, for the Lord is fighting for them against us."

The Lord said to Moses, Stretch out your hand over the sea so that the water may flow back over the Egyptians. Moses stretched out his hand over the sea, and the water returned and covered the chariots and the horsemen and swept them into the sea. Not one of them survived. But the Israelites walked through the sea on dry ground.

That day, the Lord saved Israel from the hands of the Egyptians, and the Israelites saw the Egyptians lying dead on the seashore. When the Israelites saw the great power of the Lord displayed against the Egyptians, the people feared the Lord, believed in him, and trusted his servant, Moses.

Then Moses and the children of Israel sang a song to the Lord:

"The horse and the rider have been thrown into the sea. The Lord is my strength and salvation. He is my God, my father's God, and I will exalt him. The Lord is a man of war. Pharaoh's chariots and his army sank into the bottom like stones. Your right hand shattered the enemy into pieces. You sent forth your anger, which consumed them like stubble. By the blast of your nostrils, the waters were piled up and stood like a wall. 'The enemy said I would overtake and divide the spoils. I will draw my sword and destroy them.' Who is like you, glorious in holiness and doing wonders? You stretched out your right hand, and the earth swallowed them. You have guided the people you redeemed with your strength to your holy dwelling. The people will be afraid, and sorrow will take hold of the inhabitants of Palestina. Then the dukes of Edom will be amazed, the nobles of Moab will tremble, and the inhabitants of Canaan will

melt away. Fear and dread will fall on them. By the greatness of your arm, they shall be silent as stones till the people pass over whom you have acquired. You will bring them and plant them on the mountain of your inheritance. The Lord will reign for ever and ever. When Pharaoh's horses, horsemen, and chariots went into the sea, and the Lord brought the waters again upon them, the children of Israel walked in the middle of the sea on dry ground."

And Miriam the prophetess, Aaron's sister, took a timbrel in her hand, and all the women joined her with timbrels, and they danced.

After Moses brought Israel from the Red Sea, he led the Israelites into the desert of Shur for three days without finding water. Finally, when they approached Marah, they gained hope, seeing some water. But they were disappointed after tasting the water. It was bitter, and they could not drink it. Therefore, the name of that place was called Marah. And the people grumbled against Moses dying of thirst, saying, What shall we drink? Then Moses called upon the Lord, and the Lord showed him a tree. When he threw it into the water, the water became sweet, and the Israelites were able to drink the water.

On the fifteenth day of the second month, after departing from Egypt, they reached the wilderness of Sin. This time, the people murmured against Moses and Aaron out of hunger. They said to Moses and Aaron, "You have brought us into the dessert to starve this entire assembly to death."

Then the Lord told Moses, "I will rain down bread from heaven in the morning, and the people shall go out and gather each day enough for that day. This way, I will test whether they will follow my instructions. But on the sixth day, they shall gather twice as much as they gathered on the other days. And in the evening, they will get flesh to eat."

Moses and Aaron said to the Israelites, "In the evening, you will know; it was the Lord who brought you out of Egypt, and in the morning, you will see the glory of the Lord, because he heard your complaint." The Lord said to Moses, "Tell the people, in the evening you will eat meat, and in the morning you will be filled with bread."

That evening, the quails came up and covered the camp, and in the morning, there was a layer of dew around the camp. After the dew had gone up, there lay a small round thing on the ground, and the Israelites did not know what it was. So they called it Manna (*like coriander seeds, white in colour, and tasting like wafers made with honey*). The people gathered the manna and ground it in the mill or crushed it in a mortar, baked it, and made loaves. It tasted like fresh oil.

They were told to gather an Omer (*2.3 L*) for each man according to the number of people in their tent and not to keep the remaining until the morning. However, some of them, who had kept it until the next day, found worms, and it began to smell. Each morning, everyone gathered as per their requirements, and it melted when the sun waxed hot.

On the sixth day, they gathered twice as much, with the next day being the holy sabbath. When the leaders of the community went and complained to Moses, he said, "This is what the Lord had commanded. Tomorrow is the day of the Sabbath, a holy day for the Lord. On the sixth day, bake it and keep it for the next morning. Six days you will gather it, but on the seventh day, the day of Sabbath, there will not be any."

And they kept the bread until the next morning, but it neither stank nor had any worms. The people rested on the seventh day. Some of the people who did not follow the instructions of the Lord went to gather Manna on the seventh day, but they found none. And the children of Israel ate Manna for forty years **until they reached the border of Canaan.**

Later, the children of Israel journeyed from Sin to Rephidim, where there was no water for the people to drink. They harassed Moses again, saying, You have brought us out of Egypt to kill us, our children, and our cattle with thirst. Then Moses said, "Why are you quarrelling with me and tempting the Lord? Then Moses cried to the Lord, "What am I to do with these people, because they are ready to stone me?"

The Lord said, "Go before the people, with the rod in your hand, and take some of the elders of Israel. I will stand before you on the rock in Horeb. You shall strike the rock, and water shall come out of the rock, and the people will drink." Moses did so, and he called the place Massah and Meribah because the people of Israel tested the Lord.

When the Israelites came to Rephidim, the people of Amalek attacked them. So, Moses told Joshua, "Choose some of the men and go out to fight with Amalek. And I will stand on the top of the hill with the rod of God in my hand." Joshua did as Moses had instructed him and fought with the Amalekites.

And Moses, Aaron, and Hur went to the top of the hill. When Moses held up his hand, the Israelites were winning, but whenever he let down his hand, the Amalekites were winning. When Moses hands became tired, Aaron and Hur took a stone and put it for Moses to sit on. Aaron and Hur supported the hands of Moses on either side, so that his hands were steady until the sun set. And Joshua defeated the Amalekites and their people.

Then the Lord said to Moses, "Write this in a book as a reminder, and read it aloud to Joshua, because I will erase the name of Amalek from under heaven." Moses built an altar, named it Jehovahnissi, and said the Lord would be at war against the Amalakites from generation to generation.

Now Jethro, the priest of Midian, Moses's father-in-law, heard all that the Lord had done to Moses and the children of Israel and how the Lord brought Israel out of Egypt. Jethro brought Zipporah, Moses' wife, and her two sons, Gershom and Eliezer, back to Moses, who were sent to Jethro's house. Jethro sent word to Moses on his arrival at the Mount of God, where Moses had camped.

Moses went to meet his father-in-law on the Mount of God. He bowed at Jethro and kissed him, and they asked about each other's welfare. Moses told his father-in-law all that the Lord had done to Pharaoh and the Egyptians, the hardships they came across along the way, and how the Lord rescued them. Jethro rejoiced for all the goodness that the Lord had done to the people of Israel. Jethro said, Blessed be the Lord, for the Lord is greater than all gods. **Then Aaron went with the elders of Israel to have a meal with Moses's father-in-law in the presence of God.**

The next day, Moses sat to judge the people, and the people stood around him from morning till evening to sort out any unmanageable issues among them. When Moses father-in-law saw all that Moses was doing for his people, Jethro told Moses, What you are doing is not good. You will surely become tired, for it is too heavy for you to judge and perform this task alone.

Then Jethro gave counsel to Moses to select capable men who fear God, are trustworthy, and hate covetousness (*desire for another's possession*) from all the people. Place them as rulers of thousands, hundreds, fifties, and tens. Let them judge the people at all times with smaller issues and bring to you only the greater issues they are unable to solve. This will ease your burden, and you will overcome the strain, and the people will also go in peace. Moses listened to the advice of his father-in-law and followed his suggestions. Soon after all this, Moses said good-bye to his father-in-law, who returned to his own country.

5. THE TEN COMMANDMENTS

In the third month, the children of Israel departed from Rephidim, reached the desert of Sinai, and camped in front of the mountain. Then Moses climbed the mountain to appear before the Lord, and the Lord called him from the mountain. And he said, "You know how I carried you on eagles' wings and brought you to me? If you obey me and keep my covenant, you will be my special treasure out of all nations. You will be a kingdom of priests and a holy nation. Give this message to the people of Israel."

Moses returned from the mountain, summoned the elders of the people, and told them all the words that the Lord had commanded him to speak. Then all the people responded together: "We will do everything that the Lord has commanded." Moses returned the words of the people to the Lord.

Then the Lord said to Moses, "Tell the people to sanctify today, tomorrow, and wash their clothes, and be ready on the third day, because the Lord will come down in the sight of all the people upon Mount Sinai. Warn the people not to approach the mountain or touch its boundaries. Whoever touches the mount shall surely be put to death, whether it be a beast or a man. They may approach the mountain only after hearing the trumpet sound."

Moses conveyed all the words of the Lord to the children of Israel, and they were ready. On the third day in the morning, there was thunder and lightning and a thick cloud over the mountain, and the blast of the trumpet was so loud that all the people in the camp trembled. Moses brought the people out of the camp to meet God, and they stood at the bottom of the mountain. And mountain Sinai was smoking because the Lord descended upon it in the form of fire, and the whole mountain trembled greatly. The trumpet's voice sounded long and grew louder and louder, and Moses spoke, and the voice of God answered him.

And the Lord descended on top of Mount Sinai. And he called Moses to the top of the mount, and Moses went up. He told Moses, "Go down and come up with Aaron, and even the priests who approach the Lord, sanctify themselves. And let not the people force their way through to gaze at the Lord, lest they perish."

Then Moses went down to the people and conveyed the ten commandments that the Lord told him.

THE TEN COMMANDMENTS

1. You shall have no other gods other than me.
2. You shall not make any idols for yourself of any kind.
3. You shall not misuse the name of the Lord, your God.
4. Remember the Sabbath day (*the seventh day*) by keeping it holy.
5. Honour your father and your mother.
6. You shall not murder.
7. You shall not commit adultery.
8. You shall not steal.
9. You shall not give false testimony against your neighbour.
10. You shall not covet (*desire others possessions*).

When the people saw the thunder, lightning, and the smoking mountain and heard the trumpet, they trembled with fear and moved and stood at a distance. They told Moses, You speak to us, and we will hear; but let not God speak to us, lest we die.

Moses said to the people, Fear not, for God has come to test you, so that the fear of God be with you, and you sin not. The people stood at a distance, and only Moses went near to the thick darkness where God was.

The Lord told Moses, "Tell the children of Israel, you have seen me talking with you from heaven; so you shall not make gods of silver or gold. Then come up with Aaron, Nadab, Abihu, and seventy of the elders of Israel and worship from a distance. Only you shall come near the Lord, but the others will not come near." Moses told all the words of the Lord to the people. The people replied with one voice that they would follow all the words of the Lord.

Then Moses climbed up the mountain with Aaron, Nadab, Abihu, and seventy of the elders, and they saw the God of Israel. Under his feet, they saw a paved work of sapphire stone, as bright blue as the sky. The Lord said to Moses, "Come up to the mountain and stay here; I will give you tables of stone with the law and commandments that I have written. You teach them to the children of Israel."

Moses said to the elders, Wait here for us until we come back; Aaron and Hur are with you; if anyone has a dispute, consult with them. Then Moses went with his minister, Joshua, up to the mountain of God.

After Moses went up to the mountain, the cloud covered it. And the glory of the Lord settled on the mountain for six days. On the seventh day, the Lord called Moses from the midst of the cloud. The sight of the glory of the Lord was like consuming fire on top of the mountain in the eyes of the children of Israel. And Moses entered into the midst of the cloud, and he was on the mountain forty days and forty nights. The Lord communed with Moses on Mount Sinai.

The Lord spoke to Moses, saying, Ask the children of Israel to make an Ark of shittim wood (*precious wood*) of pure gold. The length of the Ark should be two and a half cubits, the breadth one and a half cubits, and the height one and a half cubits. Overlay (*cover*) it with pure gold, inside and outside, and mould it with gold. Cast four rings of gold in the four corners of the four feet. Make poles with shittim wood covered with gold, and put the poles into the rings to carry with them. Do not remove the poles from the rings.

Make a mercy seat of pure gold, two and a half cubits in length and one and a half cubits in breadth. Make two cherubims of gold on the two ends of the mercy seat with wings stretched out high, covering the mercy seat facing each other. Put the mercy seat upon the Ark, and in the Ark, you shall put the testimony that I will give you. I will meet you and speak with you there above the mercy seat between the two cherubims regarding the commandment for the children of Israel.

Make a table of shittim wood, two cubits of length, one cubit of breadth, and one and a half cubits of height, and overlay it with pure gold. Design a border and add a golden crown to the border. Make four gold rings for the table and attach them to the four corners of the four legs close to the rim to hold the poles and carry the table. The dishes, bowls, and spoons should be made of pure gold. You shall set bread on the table before me daily. When the Lord put an end to communicating with Moses on Mount Sinai, he gave Moses two tables of testimony, made of stone and written with his finger.

In the meantime, when the people saw, that Moses had delayed coming down from the mountain, the people of Israel gathered around Aaron and said, Make us gods to lead us, for we do not know what happened to Moses. Then Aaron told the people, "Take off the gold ornaments from your wives and children and bring them to me." He then melted the gold and fashioned it into a calf.

The next day, the people rose up early in the morning, offered sacrifices, and made a feast.

Seeing that the people had turned away from following the Lord, the Lord told Moses, "Your people have corrupted themselves by worshipping the image of a calf. They are stiff-necked (*stubborn*) people; I will destroy them and make you a great nation." Then Moses told God, "Turn away from your fierce anger, change your mind, and do not bring disaster to your people. The Egyptians will say that the people of Israel were brought out of Egypt to kill them in the mountains and wipe them off the face of the earth. You had promised Abraham, Isaac, and Israel, your servants, that you would multiply their seed as the stars of heaven." Then the Lord repented of the evil that he thought and did not bring the disaster to his people.

Moses went down from the mountain with the two tables of testimony in his hand. They were written on both sides and were the graven (carved) work of God, written by God.

When Joshua heard the noise of people, he said there seemed to be something like the sound of war in the camp, and Moses replied, It is not the sound of victory, defeat, or singing that is heard. But as soon as Moses approached the camp, he saw the calf and the people dancing. Seeing that, Moses anger soared, and he threw the tables out of his hands and broke them at the foot of the mountain. And he took the calf that they had made and burned it in the fire. Then he ground it to powder, strewed (*threw all over*) it upon the water, and made the children of Israel drink of it.

Moses asked Aaron, what did these people do to you that you have brought a great sin upon them? Then Aaron said, do not be angry. The people said, "We do not know what happened to Moses, who brought us from the land of Egypt; make gods for us. So, I asked the people to give their gold, and I made calf out of it."

The next day, Moses said to the people, You have committed a great sin. I will go up to the Lord and make an atonement (*reconciliation*) for your sin. And Moses returned to the Lord and said, the people have sinned greatly and made themselves gods of gold; forgive their sin, or else erase me out of the book that you have written. Then the Lord replied, whoever has sinned against me, I will erase them out of my book. You go and lead the people, and my angel shall go before you. Then the Lord struck the people with plague because they worshipped the calf that Aaron made.

Moses pitched a tabernacle (*a temporary place of worship*) far off from the camp and called it the tabernacle of the congregation for meetings. People who sought the Lord went to the tabernacle. Whenever Moses went into the tabernacle, all the people stood up at their tent doors, watching him until he entered the tent. When Moses entered the tent, the pillar of cloud descended and stood at the entrance of the tent. And when the people saw the pillar of cloud, they stood up and worshipped from the entrance of their tent. The Lord would speak to Moses' face-to-face, as one speaks to a friend.

One day, Moses said to the Lord, "You have been telling me to lead these people, but you have not let me know whom you will send with me. You have said, 'I know you by name'. If you are pleased with me, teach me your ways."

The Lord replied, "My presence will go with you, and I will give you rest. I will do what you have asked, because I am pleased with you and I know you by name."

Then Moses said to the Lord, If I have found grace in your sight, show me your glory. Then the Lord said, You cannot see my face, for no man shall live after seeing me. Then the Lord said, "There is a place near me where you may stand upon a rock. And when my glory passes by, I will put you in a cleft (*an opening or split*) of the rock and cover you with my hand until I have passed by. Then I will take away my hand, and you shall see my back, but you will not be able to see my face.

The Lord told Moses, "Chisel out two tables of stone tablets like the first one, and I will write upon these tables the words that were in the first tables that you broke. Come up to the top of Mount Sinai in the morning and present yourself to me. None of them shall come up with you, and none of them should be seen throughout all the mountains; not even the herds or flocks should grace the mountain.

So, Moses chiselled two tables of stone like the first ones, as the Lord had commanded, and went the next morning to Mount Sinai. He carried the two tables of stones in his hand. And the Lord descended in a cloud and stood with Moses. And he proclaimed the name of the Lord. Then the Lord passed by before Moses and proclaimed (*announced or declared*) the Lord, "The Lord God, merciful and gracious, longsuffering and abundant in goodness and truth, keeping mercy for thousands, forgiving wickedness, rebellion, and sin. He punishes the children and their children for the sin of their parents to the third and fourth generations." Moses quickly bowed his head and worshipped.

The Lord told Moses, "Write all the words that I tell you, with which I have made a covenant with you and with Israel." Moses was there with the Lord for forty days and forty nights. He neither ate bread nor drank water. He wrote on the tables of stone the words of the covenant, the ten commandments.

When Moses came down from Mount Sinai with the two tables of testimony in his hand, he was not aware that the skin of his face was radiant and shining. And when Aaron and the children of Israel saw Moses, they were afraid to go near him, for his face was shining. Moses called Aaron, the elders, and the people of Israel to come near him. He put a veil on his face until he finished speaking with the people. When Moses went before the Lord to speak with him, he took the veil off. He would put on the veil again until he went to speak with the Lord, because his face was shining. He told the people all that the Lord had spoken with him on Mount Sinai.

6. BIBLICAL MEAT AND ANOINTMENT

Moses gathered the whole Israelite community, and he conveyed the words of the Lord to them. "For six days, you will work, but on the seventh day, you shall not do any work, for it is a holy day, and do not light a fire in your dwelling place."

Moses told the children of Israel: Whoever is of a willing heart, let them bring an offering to the Lord of gold, silver, brass, precious stones, anointing oil, sweet incense (*perfume*), linen, durable leather, shittim wood, and other accessories for the work of the tabernacle.

So the children of Israel brought to the Lord all the offerings that the Lord had commanded through Moses to set up the tabernacle. Moses said to the children of Israel, "The Lord has chosen Bezaleel, the son of Uri, from the tribe of Judah, and Aholiab from the tribe of Dan, and every wise-hearted man who was filled with the spirit of God in wisdom, understanding, knowledge, and all manner of workmanship in gold, silver, and brass." They were artistic designers of all kinds of crafts and worked as engravers.

Moses summoned Bezaleel, Oholiab, and the other specially gifted persons whom the Lord had given the ability to and were willing to build the sanctuary (*sacred area*). They received all the offerings from Moses that the Israelites had donated to construct the sanctuary. The craftsmen told Moses the Israelites had brought more than enough materials. So Moses commanded the people not to bring any more offerings, and the people stopped bringing them.

The children of Israel did all the work according to all that the Lord had commanded Moses. Moses inspected all their work and was content with what was done, and Moses blessed them.

The Lord told Moses, "Set up the tabernacle of the tent on the first day of the first month. Place the ark of the testimony in the tabernacle and cover the ark with a curtain. Take the anointing oil and anoint the tabernacle and all its furnishings, and it will be holy."

"Bring Aaron and his sons to the entrance of the tabernacle and wash them with water. Dress Aaron in holy garments, anoint him, and consecrate (*make holy*) him to serve me as priest. Cloth and anoint Aaron's sons, Eleazar and Ithamar, just as you anointed their father to serve me as priests." They were anointed to be priests throughout their generations.

Moses finished all the things just as the Lord commanded him. Moses, Aaron, and his sons washed their hands and feet whenever they entered or approached the tabernacle, as the Lord commanded Moses.

Then a cloud covered the tabernacle, and it was filled with the glory of the Lord, and Moses was unable to enter the tabernacle. The Israelites set out on their journey when the cloud was lifted and did not set out when the cloud was not lifted. The cloud of the Lord was above the tabernacle during the day, and from evening until morning it appeared like fire.

The Lord told Moses and Aaron to speak to the children of Israel regarding the beasts they should eat and the beasts they should not eat on earth.

Of the land, you shall eat every animal with cloven hooves (*the tip of the toe*), with the hoof split into two parts, and that chews the cud. They are the ox, sheep, goat, deer, gazelle (*an Asian animal that runs at high speed*), wild goat, and antelope (*African mammals*).

You shall not eat the animals like the camel, coney (*rabbit*), or swine, for they chew the cud but do not have cloven hooves. You shall not eat their flesh or touch their dead carcasses. Whatever goes on his paws is unclean.

In the water, any kind of fish that has fins and scales may be eaten. Anything that lives in the water and does not have fins and scales is unclean.

Of the fowls, you shall not eat the eagle, the ossifrage (*young of the sea eagle*), and the osprey (*bird that feeds on fish and has narrow wings*), like the vulture, kite, raven, owl, hawk, cuckoo, ostrich, bat, cormorant (*medium to large black seabird's family*), swan, pelican, stork, heron, jackdaw (belongs to the crow family), lapwing (*wading birds*), fowl that creep and yet they can fly, and those that have legs above their feet to leap upon the earth.

All the winged insects are unclean, except those that can hop. You may eat the locusts, beetles, and grasshoppers of his kind.

Creeping things that creep upon the earth, like the weasel (*a carnivorous mammal*), the mouse, the tortoise, the ferret (*like the weasel*), the chameleon, the lizard, the snail, and the mole *(a rat family)*, are unclean. Whoever moves upon the belly and that which goes upon four feet or has more feet, you shall not eat.

The Lord told Moses to speak to the children of Israel to observe all the statutes:

- Be holy, for I, the Lord, your God, am holy.
- Everyone must respect their father and mother.
- Do not turn to idols or make any metal images.
- When you reap the harvest of your land, do not reap until the edges of the field or gather the gleanings (*leftovers after the harvest*) of your harvest.
- Do not pick up every grape in your vineyard. You shall leave them for the poor and strangers.
- Do not steal or lie to one another.
- Do not swear falsely by my name.
- Do not rob your neighbour or rob the wages of a hired worker.
- Do not curse the deaf or put a stumbling block before the blind.
- Do not disrespect the poor or show favouritism towards the person of the mighty.

- ➢ You shall not act as a talebearer (*person who spreads gossip*).
- ➢ You will not hate your brother.
- ➢ Do not seek revenge or bear any grudge (*ill will about someone*), but love your neighbour.
- ➢ Do not eat any meat with blood.
- ➢ Do not cut your flesh for the dead or put tattoo marks on yourselves.
- ➢ Do not seek the wizards (*magical practices*) to defile yourself.
- ➢ Rise up before an elderly person and respect them.
- ➢ Love the foreigner who resides in your land, for you were strangers in the land of Egypt.
- ➢ You shall be righteous while measuring the weight.

"If you follow my laws and obey my commandments, I will send you rain in due season, and the land will yield her crops and the trees their fruit. If you forsake my statutes and reject my judgements, I will punish you seven times more for your sins. I will break down your power of pride and make your heavens as iron and your earth as brass."

The Lord told Moses to take the sum of the whole community, of the children of Israel, by the house of their fathers, from twenty years old and upward, who are able to go to war. With you, there shall be one man from each tribe, the head of his family. These are the names that will stand with you. Elizur from the tribe of Reuben; Shelumiel of Simeon; Nahshon of Judah; Nethaneel of Issachar; Eliab of Zebulun, of the children of Joseph; Elishama of Ephraim and Gamaliel of Manasseh; Abidan of Benjamin; Ahiezer of Dan; Pagiel of Asher; Eliasaph of Gad; and Ahira of Naphtali. The Lord commanded Moses not to number the tribe of Levi. He told the Levites to keep charge of the tabernacle of the testimony and all the vessels and things that belong to it.

These are the names of the sons of Aaron: Nadab, the firstborn, Abihu, Eleazer, and Ithamar. Nadab and Abihu died before the

Lord because they offered unauthorised fire before the Lord in the wilderness of Mount Sinai, which the Lord had not commanded them. So the fire went out from the Lord and consumed them, and they died. They did not have any children.

Then Moses said to Aaron and his sons, Eleazar and Ithamar, "Do not uncover your heads or tear your clothes, or you will die, because the Lord's anointing oil is on you." Eleazer and Ithamar ministered in the priest's office, in the sight of Aaron, their father. The Lord told Moses, "Present the tribe of Levi before Aaron to minister to him. They shall take care of all the instruments of the tabernacle and be in charge of the children of Israel to do the service of the tabernacle."

Moses had fully set up the tabernacle and anointed and sanctified all the instruments and vessels of the tabernacle. Then the heads of the house, who were princes of the tribes, brought their offerings before the Lord. The Lord said to Moses, "Men from twenty-five years old and upward will do the service of the tabernacle and retire to do the service at the age of fifty years. But they shall assist their brothers in performing their duties."

The children of Israel journeyed not; whether it was two days, a month, or one year, they remained in their tents when the cloud stayed for a longer period upon the tabernacle. By the command of the Lord, they camped, and by his command, they set out on their journey. They obeyed the Lord's order through Moses.

The Lord told Moses to make two silver trumpets and use them to call the community together and to set out on their journey. When one trumpet was blown, the leaders of Israel were assembled, and when both were blown, the whole community was assembled. With the trumpet blasting once, the tribe of the east set out, and on the second blast, the tribe of the south set out. Aaron's sons, the priests, blew the trumpets.

On the twentieth day of the second month of the second year, the cloud lifted from above the tabernacle. The Israelites then journeyed from Mount Sinai and reached the desert of Paran, where the cloud rested.

The division of the camp set out on their journey and marched as per the Lord's command through Moses for the first time. The first was the tribe of Judah, followed by the others, and the last was the tribe of Naphtali.

Now Moses said to Hobab, the son of Jethro (Moses' father-in-law), to accompany them to the land that the Lord had promised. Initially, Hobab refused but agreed after Moses's request. Moses told Hobab, "You know where to camp in the desert, and you can be our eyes. If you go with us, we will share the good things the Lord gives us." Then they departed from the mount of the Lord on a three-day journey, and the ark of the Lord went before them in search of a resting place. The cloud of the Lord was upon them by day when they set out of the camp.

The people started complaining, and they wept for meat, comparing the food they ate in Egypt, like the fish, cucumbers, melons, leeks, onions, and garlic. They said, Now we have lost our appetite since there is nothing to eat other than the manna.

Moses heard the people wailing at the door of their tent. Moses was displeased, and the Lord was also angry. And Moses asked the Lord, "Why have you laid the burden of all these people upon me? Did I conceive all these people to carry them in my bosom as a nursing father to the land you promised? I am not able to bear these people alone; it is too heavy for me. I pray that you kill me if I have found favour in your sight."

The Lord said to Moses, "Bring seventy elders, known to you as leaders, and officials to the tent, that they may stand with you. I will come down and speak with you there, and I will take some of the spirit from you and put it on them. This way, they will share the burden of the people with you.

Say to the people, "sanctify yourselves, for tomorrow you will eat flesh. You will not eat it just for one day, two days, five days, ten days, or twenty days. But you will eat for a whole month, until it comes out of your nostrils, because you have rejected the Lord."

Then Moses said to the Lord, "Six hundred thousand (600,000) men are with me. Even if the flocks and herds were slaughtered, or if the fish in the sea were gathered, will it suffice them?" The Lord said, "Is the Lord's arm too short? You will see whether it comes true or not."

So Moses brought the seventy of the elders and made them stand around the tabernacle. Then the Lord came down in a cloud, spoke to Moses, and took some of the spirit from Moses and gave it to the seventy elders. When the spirit rested upon them, they prophesied.

Then there went forth a wind that brought quails from the sea. The people stood all that day and night, and all the next day they gathered the quails. He who gathered the least gathered ten homers (*one homer = 220 litres*). While the meat was yet between their teeth, the anger of the Lord struck the people with a very great plague. They named the place Kibroth Hattaavah because they buried the dead there. And the people travelled from Kibroth Hattaavah to Hazeroth.

Now Aaron and Miriam began to talk against Moses, saying, Has the Lord spoken only through Moses? Did not he speak through us also? And the Lord heard this. (*Moses was a very meek man above all men upon the face of the earth.*) The Lord spoke suddenly to Moses, Aaron, and Miriam, "Come out, the three of you, to the tabernacle." And the three of them went out. Then the Lord came down in a pillar of cloud. He stood at the entrance of the tabernacle and called Aaron and Miriam, and they both went forward. The Lord said, "Listen to my words; my servant Moses is faithful in all my house. With him, I will speak face-to-face, clearly, and not in riddles. He sees the form of the Lord. Then why were you not afraid to speak against my servant Moses?"

The anger of the Lord arose against them, and he departed. Then the cloud departed from the tabernacle, and Miriam became leprous, white as snow. When Aaron saw that Miriam was leprous, he told Moses, "My Lord, we have done foolishly and have sinned; please do not let her flesh look half consumed and do not bestow the sin upon us."

So Moses cried to the Lord, "I beg of you, heal her now." The Lord replied to Moses, "If her father spat on her face, should not she be ashamed? Let her be shut outside the camp for seven days, and after that, she can be brought back." So Miriam was shut out of the camp for seven days, and the people discontinued their journey until she was brought again into the camp. After that, the people moved and camped in the desert of Paran.

7. KORAH THE REBEL

Moses then sent one head from each tribe to explore the land of Canaan, as the Lord had commanded. The names from each tribe were Shammua from the tribe of Reuben, Shaphat from Simeon, Caleb from Judah, Igal from Issachar, Oshea from Ephraim, Palti from Benjamin, Gaddiel from Zebulun, Gaddi from Joseph, Ammiel from Dan, Sethur from Asher, Nahbi from Nephtali, and Geuel from Gad.

Moses had sent them to spy on the land of Canaan to see if the people there were strong or weak, few or many in number, if the land was good or bad, whether they lived in tents or well-built houses, and if the land was fertile or not. And he told them to bring the fruit of the land, as it was the season for the first ripe grapes.

So they went and explored throughout the land and reached Hebron, where Ahiman, Sheshai, and Talmai, the children of Anak, lived. Then they reached a valley, and from there they cut down a branch with a single cluster of grapes, and two people carried it on a pole between them. They also took some pomegranates and figs, and they called that place the Valley of Eschol. They returned to Kadesh in the desert of Paran after forty days, to Moses, Aaron, and the community of Israel. And they showed them the fruits of the land and reported to them, "Surely the land flows with milk and honey. But the people who lived there were strong; the cities were walled and very large; and moreover, they saw the children of Anak."

Then Caleb said, "Let us go at once and possess the land." But the men that went with him said, "We cannot attack those people, for they are stronger than us and men of good stature (great *height and size*). There we saw the sons of Anak, who were like giants. And we seemed like grasshoppers in our own eyes, and we looked the same in their sight as well."

Hearing this, all the people wept aloud the whole night and grumbled against Moses and Aaron. The whole assembly said, "It would have been better for us to have died in Egypt. Why has the Lord brought us here to fall by the sword? Our wives and children will be taken as prey. Wouldn't it be better to return to Egypt? Let us choose a leader and go back to Egypt."

Then Moses and Aaron fell face down in front of the whole Israelites gathered there. Caleb, son of Jephunneh, and Joshua, son of Nun, who were among those who explored the land, tore their clothes and told the children of Israel, "The land is exceedingly good. If the Lord is pleased with us, he will take us to the land flowing with milk and honey and give it to us. Only do not rebel against the Lord. Do not fear the people of the land; the

Lord is with us." But the whole assembly talked about stoning them.

Then the glory of the Lord appeared in the tabernacle before all the Israelites. And the Lord said to Moses, "How long will these people provoke me? I will strike them with plague, disown them, and make a greater and mightier nation of you than them." Then Moses said to the Lord, If you kill all these people, then the Egyptians will hear it. And the other nations that have heard the fame of you will speak, saying, "Because the Lord was not able to take these people into the land that he swore unto them, he has killed them in the wilderness. The Lord is patient, of great mercy, and forgiving of the wicked and rebellion. Yet he punishes the children for the sins of their parents up to the third and fourth generations. Forgive these people because your love is great, as you have pardoned them from the time they left Egypt until now."

The Lord replied, "I have forgiven them according to your word. All those who have seen my glory and miracles yet have not heard my voice, provoked me, and tested me ten times will not see the land that I swore. But I will take Caleb, my servant, who has a different spirit and follows me wholeheartedly, to the land. And his descendants will inherit it."

The Lord said, "Since this wicked community grumbled against me, everyone who is twenty years old and older will not enter the land I swore, except Caleb, son of Jephunneh, and Joshua, son of Nun." The men who were responsible for spreading the bad report about the land were struck and died of plague before the Lord. Only Joshua and Caleb survived.

Moses conveyed all that happened to the Israelites, and they mourned bitterly. Next morning, the people set out for the highest point of the hill, saying, Now we are ready to go up to the land the Lord promised, for we have sinned.

"But Moses said, Why are you disobeying the Lord's command? You will not succeed. Do not go, because the Lord is not with you. You will be defeated and fall to the sword by your enemies, the Amalekites and the Canaanites, since you have turned away from the Lord."

But they refused to adhere to the words of Moses and went up to the top of the hill without Moses and the Ark of the Lord's Covenant. Then the Amalekites and the Canaanites, who lived on the hill, attacked and beat them down all the way to Hormah.

Moses called for Dathan and Abiram, the sons of Eliab, but they refused to come, saying, You want to be prince over us altogether. Moreover, you have not taken us to the land flowing with milk and honey or given us any inheritance of fields and vineyards. Then Moses was angry and said to the Lord, Do not accept their offering, for I have not hurt them nor taken anything from them.

There was Korah, the son of Izhar, from Levi's tribe, and Dathan and Abiram from the tribe of Reuben, who gathered two hundred and fifty (*250*) Israelites, princes, community leaders, and celebrity men. They went as a group against Moses and Aaron. They accused Moses and Aaron and said, "The whole congregation is holy, and the Lord is among them; then why are you exalting yourselves above the congregation of the Lord?" Hearing this, Moses fell down on his face. Then Moses said to Korah and all his company, "Tomorrow, the Lord will show who is holy."

Moses said to Korah, "You and all your followers, and Aaron, have to appear before the Lord tomorrow. Then Moses proposed a test to Korah, his company, and Aaron. Moses said, "Each man has to take incensed censers (*containers for burning incense*) with fire and place them before the Lord, two hundred and fifty censors (250), and Aaron also. The next day, every man took his censer, put fire and incense in it, and stood at the door of the tabernacle with Moses and Aaron. Korah gathered his men to the tabernacle, and the glory of the Lord appeared to all.

And the Lord spoke to Moses and Aaron, "Separate yourselves from among this entire assembly, that I may put an end to them in a moment." Then Moses and Aaron fell face down and cried, "O God, the breath of all living things, will your anger be on the whole assembly for the sin of one man?"

Then the Lord said to Moses, Tell the assembly to move away from the tents of Korah, Dathan, and Abiram. So Moses rushed to Dathan and Abiram, followed by the elders of Israel, and told them, "Get away from the tents of these wicked men and do not touch anything of theirs. If you do so, you will be destroyed for their sins." So, all the people got out of the tent of Korah, Dathan, and Abiram. Dathan and Abiram also went out with their wives, children, and little ones and stood at the entrance of their tents.

Then Moses said, "By this, you will know that the Lord sent me to do these things, for I have not done them from my own mind. If these men die the natural death of all men, then the Lord has not sent me. But if the Lord does something totally new and the earth opens her mouth and swallows them with everything that belongs to them, then you will understand that these men have provoked the Lord."

As soon as Moses finished speaking these words, the ground suddenly split open beneath them. And the earth opened her mouth and swallowed them, along with their households and all those associated with Korah, together with their possessions. They went down alive into the pit with everything they owned, and the earth closed upon them. They perished among the people of Israel. Seeing this, all the other Israelites who were around them fled, saying, "The earth will swallow us too." Then a fire came out from the Lord, and the two hundred and fifty people (*250*) who offered incense were burned.

As instructed by the Lord, Moses told Eleazar, the son of Aaron, "Remove the censers from the charred remains and scatter the coals some distance away. Since the censers are holy, collect the bronze censers and make broad plates out of them as a covering for the altar. This will remind the Israelites and warn them that no one except a descendant of Aaron should enter the Lord's presence to burn incense, or else he will become like Korah and his followers."

The next day, all the children of Israel gathered and murmured against Moses and Aaron, saying, "You have killed the people of the Lord." But it so happened that, when the people were gathered in opposition to Moses and Aaron, they turned towards the tabernacle, and suddenly the cloud covered it and the glory of the Lord appeared. Then Moses and Aaron appeared before the tabernacle of the congregation. And the Lord spoke to Moses, "Get away from this assembly, that I may consume them in a moment."

Then Moses told Aaron, "Take the censer, put fire in it, put incense, and take it quickly to the congregation and make an atonement (*reconcile*) to the Lord, for the Lord is angry and the plague has begun." So Aaron took the censer with incense, as Moses had commanded, ran into the midst of the congregation, and made atonement. But the plague had already begun among the people.

Aaron offered the incense and made atonement for them. He stood between the dead and the living, and the plague stopped. Those that died in the plague were fourteen thousand and seven hundred (*14,700*), beside the people that died because of Korah. After the plague was stopped, Aaron returned to Moses, to the door of the tabernacle of the congregation.

In the first month, the whole Israelite population arrived in the desert of Zin, and they stayed in Kadesh. Miriam, Aaron's sister, died and was buried there.

Now there was no water for the community, and the people quarrelled with Moses. "Why have you brought us into the wilderness so that we and our livestock should die? In this place, there are no grains, figs, grapevines, or pomegranates, nor is there water to drink."

Then Moses and Aaron went out of the presence of the people to the tabernacle's door and fell upon their faces, and the glory of the Lord appeared to them. And the Lord spoke to Moses, "You and Aaron, take the rod, gather the people together, and speak to the rock before their eyes, and it shall give water. Moses and Aaron gathered the congregation before the rock. "Listen, you rebels, must we bring water out of this rock?" Moses then lifted his hand with the rod and struck the rock twice with the rod. The water came out abundantly, and they and their beasts drank the water. But the Lord said to Moses and Aaron, "Because you did not believe me, you shall not take this congregation into the land that I have given them. The water was called Meribah since the children of Israel contended with the Lord.

Moses sent messengers to the king of Edom, requesting that the king allow them to pass through his country. "We will not go through any field or vineyard or drink water from any well. We will not turn to the left or right; we will only travel along the highway through your territory." But the king of Edom did not allow them to pass through; he said, "We will attack if you try."

The children of Israel journeyed from Kadesh to Mount Hor. There, by the coast of Edom, the Lord spoke to Moses and Aaron: "Aaron will be gathered to his people. He will not enter the land that I have given the children of Israel because he rebelled against my word at the water of Meribah."The Lord told Moses, "Bring Aaron and Eleazar, his son, to Mount Hor, strip Aaron of his garments, and put them on his son Eleazar." Moses did as the Lord had commanded, and Aaron died on the top of the mountain when he was one hundred and twenty-three years old. He died in the fortieth year, on the first day of the fifth month after the children of Israel left Egypt. The children of Israel mourned the death of Aaron for thirty days.

Likewise, in the city of Heshbon, Sihon, the king of Amorites, also did not allow the children of Israel to pass through his border when Israel sent messengers and requested to pass through Sihon. He gathered all his people and went against Israel into the wilderness to fight. The Israelites defeated the Amorites and possessed their lands and cities. The children of Israel passed by the way of Bashan, and Og, the king of Bashan, went against the Israelites to battle. But the Lord said to Moses, "Fear not, for I have delivered him and his people into your hand." So the Israelites defeated them and possessed their land.

8. BALAAM'S TALKING DONKEY

The children of Israel journeyed and camped
on the plains of Moab, on the side of Jordan.

Balak, the son of Zippor, the king of the Moabites, saw all that Israel had done to the Amorites and was greatly afraid and distressed because of the children of Israel. The elders of Moab told the elders of Midian, "The children of Israel will lick up all that is around us, as the ox licks the grass of the field."

Balak, the son of Zippor, sent messengers to call Balaam, the son of Beor, saying, "There have come these people from Egypt who are mighty and cover the face of the earth. Now come and curse these people for me. For whoever you bless is blessed, and whoever you curse is cursed." So the elders of Moab and Midian went to Balaam and spoke to him the words of Balak.

Balaam told them to spend that night with him. He said, "I will report back to you with the answer the Lord gives me." And Balak's messenger's stayed with Balaam. Balaam said the word of Balak's messengers to the Lord. Then God said to Balaam, "You shall not go with them and curse those people, because they are blessed."

The next day, Balaam said to the Princes of Balak, "You go to your own country, for the Lord has refused to go with you." Then the Princes of Moab returned to Balak and said, "Balaam refused to come with us."

Balak sent again more princes and more honourable men than the previous one. They told Balaam the words of Balak: "I will promote you to very great honour, and I will do whatsoever you say to me; therefore, I pray that you come and curse the children of Israel." Then Balaam answered to the servants of Balak: Even if Balak gives me his house full of silver and gold, I cannot go beyond the word of the Lord my God to do anything great or small. He told the men, "Spend the night here, and I will find out if the Lord has anything else to say."

God appeared to Balaam that night and said, "Since the men have come to call you, go with them, but you will do only what I tell you." Balaam got up the next morning, saddled his donkey, and went with the princes of Moab. Balaam was riding on his donkey, and his two servants were with him.

On the way, the donkey saw the angel of the Lord standing with a sword drawn in his hand. Seeing the angel, the donkey turned aside, got out of the way, and went into the field. Balaam then beat the donkey to turn her in the right direction.

But the angel of the Lord stood in the path of the vineyards, and there were walls on either side. Seeing the angel of the Lord, the donkey thrust herself against the wall and crushed Balaam's foot against the wall. Balaam beat the donkey again. The angel of the Lord further moved ahead and stood in a narrow place where there was no way to turn either to the right or the left. When the donkey saw the angel of the Lord, she fell down under Balaam. And Balaam's anger was aroused, and he beat the donkey with a staff (*a long, thick wooden stick*).

Then the Lord opened the mouth of the donkey, and she said to Balaam, "What have I done to you that you have beaten me these three times?" Balaam answered the donkey, "Because you have made a fool of me, I would have killed you right now if I had a sword in my hand."

The donkey told Balaam, "Am I not the donkey that you have been riding on me ever since you owned me? Have I ever done this before?" Balaam said no. Then the Lord opened the eyes of Balaam, and he saw the angel of the Lord standing in the way with the sword in his hand. Balaam bowed his head and fell on his face.

And the angel of the Lord asked Balaam, "Why did you beat your donkey those three times? I blocked your way because your path is perverse (*evil*). The donkey saw me and turned aside from me three times. If she had not turned away from me, I would have killed you and saved her life." Balaam said to the angel of the Lord, "I have sinned, and I did not know that you stood on the way. If it displeases (*dislikes*) you, I will go back." Then the angel of the Lord said to Balaam, Go with the men, but speak only the word that I shall speak to you. So Balaam went with the princes of Balak.

When Balak heard that Balaam had come, he went to meet Balaam. Balak said to Balaam, "I had sent you an urgent invitation; then why did you not come? Am I not able to honour you?" Balaam replied, "I have come to you now, but I do not have any power to say anything I please; I must speak only the word that God puts in my mouth."

Balak took Balaam to Kirjath Huzoth. And the next morning, Balak took Balaam up to the high places of Baal. Then the Lord put a word in Balaam's mouth. And Balaam spoke, "Balak brought me to curse Jacob and defy Israel, but how will I curse whom God has not cursed, or how will I condemn when the Lord has not condemned? The children of Israel shall dwell alone, and who can count the descendants of Jacob?

Balak said to Balaam, "What have you done to me? I brought you to curse my enemies; instead, you have blessed them altogether." Then Balaam replied, "Should I not regard that which the Lord put in my mouth?"

Then Balak took Balaam to another place, the field of Zophin, at the top of Pisgah. Balaam made Balak stand there while he went to meet the Lord yonder (*at a distance*). And the Lord met Balaam and put words in his mouth to say thus: "Balak, now listen, God is not a man that he should lie, nor the son of a human being to change his mind. Will he not do what he says? I have received the command to bless; God has blessed, and I cannot reverse it. There is neither iniquity (*wickedness*) in Jacob nor any wrong against Israel. The Lord, their God, is with them. They rise up as a great lion." Then Balak said to Balaam, Neither curse them nor bless them.

Balak took Balaam to a different place, to the top of Peor. There, Balaam turned his face towards the wilderness and saw the Israelites abiding in their tents according to their tribes. Then the spirit of God came upon Balaam, and he said, "Balaam, the son of Beor, speaks, whose eyes are opened: How goodly are thy tents, Jacob? Your dwelling places are like valleys spread out and gardens by the riverside. Like the aloes (*costly, sweet-smelling wood*) planted by the Lord and cedar trees (*having needle-shaped leaves*) beside the waters. They are watered abundantly. Their kingdom shall be exalted. They have the strength of a unicorn (*a beast resembling a horse or deer with a single horn projecting from its forehead*) to devour their enemies, break their bones, and pierce them with their arrows. Blessed are they that bless you, and cursed are they that curse you."

Then Balak's anger was aroused, and he struck his hands together and said, "I called you to curse my enemies, but you have blessed them these three times. Therefore, now flee to your place. I promised to honour you greatly, but the Lord has kept you from being honoured." Balaam answered, "Did not I speak to your messengers that if Balak gives me his house full of silver and gold, I cannot go beyond the word of the Lord to do either good or evil of my own accord? I must speak what the Lord says." Then Balaam returned to his place, and Balak also went his way.

9. TEACHINGS OF MOSES

One day the Lord said to Moses, "Climb up to Mount Abarim and see the land which I have given the children of Israel. After you have seen it, you too will die like your brother Aaron, since you both disobeyed against my command at the waters of Meribah." Then Moses told the Lord, "Appoint a man over this community to lead the children of Israel. Let them not be like sheep without a shepherd."

So, the Lord said to Moses, "Choose Joshua, the son of Nun, in whom the spirit of God is, and lay your hands upon him. Present him before Eleazar, the priest, and before the whole community, and give him charge in their presence. Transfer some of your authority to Joshua so that the entire assembly will obey him." And Moses did as the Lord had commanded him.

Now the children of Reuben and Gad had a very large number of livestock. And when they saw the land of Jazer and the land of Gilead as ideal places for livestock, they went to Moses, Eleazer, the priest, and the leaders of the community. Reuben and Gad said, "If we have found grace in your sight, let this land be given to us for a possession for livestock. Do not take us over to Jordan."

Then Moses said to the children of Reuben and Gad, "Should your brothers go to war while you sit here? Why do you discourage the Israelites from going over to the land that the Lord has given them? Your ancestors also discouraged the Israelites when they went to the valley of Eshcol, which the Lord had given them. So the Lord's anger was aroused that day, and he swore that except Caleb, the son of Jephunneh, and Joshua, the son of Nun, who have followed the Lord wholeheartedly, none of them from twenty years old and above shall see the land that I swore to Abraham, Isaac, and Jacob. The Lord made the Israelites wander in the wilderness for forty years until all the people who did evil in the sight of the Lord were dead."

"Look here; you are a brood of sinners risen in the place of your fathers, increasing the anger of the Lord even more. If you turn away from following the Lord, he will once again leave these people in the wilderness, and you will destroy all these people."

Then Reuben and Gad approached Moses and told him, "We would like to build sheepfolds (*an enclosure for keeping sheep*) for our cattle and dwelling places for our little ones. After that, we will go armed for war. We will not return until the children of Israel have received their inheritance.

Moses said unto them, "If you will go armed over Jordan and drive out the enemies, you will be guiltless before the Lord; this land shall be in your possession. But if you do not do so, you will sin against the Lord." Moses told them, "Build cities for your little ones and sheepfolds for your sheep, but do what you have promised." And the children of Gad and Reuben agreed as per the Lord's commandment through Moses.

The Lord said to Moses, Divide the inheritance according to the number of members in a family. Families with more members shall be given a greater inheritance, and families with fewer members shall be given a lesser inheritance. Eleazar the priest and Joshua the son of Nun shall divide the land of inheritance by selecting one prince from every tribe.

One day Moses told the children of Israel; I pleaded with the Lord, saying, "You have begun to show your servant greatness and a strong hand. Lord, I pray, let me go over and see the land that is beyond Jordan, that pleasant mountain, and Lebanon. Because of you, the Lord was angry with me and would not listen to me. He said, Do not speak to me any more regarding this matter. Go to the top of Pisgah and see westward, northward, eastward, and southward with your eyes, since you shall not go over this Jordan. But encourage and strengthen Joshua, for he shall go over before the children of Israel to inherit the land."

Then Moses said, Now Israel, listen to me, the laws and judgements, which I teach you, that your days may be prolonged, to go and possess the land of the Lord.

These are the statutes and judgements that Moses taught to the children of Israel as commanded by the Lord:

> ➢ You shall not grave the image in the form of any figure: male, female, beast, bird, creeping things, or any fish and become corrupt.

- ➢ The Lord your God is the God of gods, the Lord of lords, a great, mighty, and terrible God. He does not discriminate against people or take rewards.
- ➢ When you look up at the sky and see the sun, moon, and stars, do not get attracted to bow down to them and worship the things that the Lord has given to all the people below the heavens as heritage.
- ➢ Your God is merciful; he will not forsake you or destroy you if you are obedient to his voice.
- ➢ The Lord made a covenant with us, who are alive here today, and not with our ancestors. Out of the heavens, he made you hear his voice to instruct you. On earth, he showed you his great fire, and you heard his words face-to-face from the midst of the fire. And I stood between the Lord and you, for you were afraid and did not go up to the mountain.
- ➢ Since he loved your fathers, he chose their descendants and brought you out of Egypt with his mighty power.

Therefore, there is no other God in the heavens above and beneath the earth other than the Lord God. You shall love the Lord thy God with all your heart, soul, and strength, and teach them diligently (*dedicatedly and carefully*) to your children.

- ➢ After the Lord has brought you to the land that he swore, your home will be full of good things that you did not have: wells dug that you did not dig, vineyards, and olive groves that you did not plant. When you have eaten and are full, do not forget the Lord, who brought you forth out of the land of Egypt from the house of slavery.
- ➢ You shall do that which is right and good in the sight of the Lord.
- ➢ When your son asks the meaning of the testimonies, statutes, and judgements that the Lord has commanded, you shall say, "We were slaves of Pharaoh in Egypt, and he brought us out of Egypt. The Lord showed signs and wonders great and terrible to Pharaoh and his people before our eyes. He

commanded us to obey all the statutes for our good always and to preserve us alive."

➢ You are holy and special people to the Lord, your God. The Lord set his love upon you because he loved you and kept the oath that he swore to your fathers.

➢ The Lord will bless the fruit of your womb and the crops of your land with fruits, wheat, barley, oil, figs, and honey. None of you will be childless among you and your livestock.

➢ He will take away all diseases and protect Israel from all the terrible diseases that occurred in Egypt, but he will inflict them upon all of them that hate you.

➢ He fed you with manna that neither you nor your ancestors knew. He made you understand that man does not live by bread alone but by every word that proceeds from the mouth of the Lord. In these forty years, neither did your clothing wear out nor did your feet swell.

- He loved the strangers by giving them food and clothing. Therefore, you also love the stranger, for you were strangers in the land of Egypt.
- Whatever I command you, observe to do it; neither add nor diminish from it.
- Be sure to set aside a tenth of all that your fields produce for the Lord, your God.
- Among you, if one of your fellow Israelites is poor within your gates, do not be hard-hearted or tight-fisted towards them. Rather, be open-handed and lend them freely whatever they need.
- You shall perform that which has gone out of your lips and keep up the promise that you have vowed to the Lord.
- Hear the voice of the Lord, thy God, that he sets you high above all nations of the earth. You will be blessed in the city and in the country. Blessed shall be your womb, your crops, your land, your livestock, the flocks of your sheep, and

your store. You will be blessed when you go out and come.

> Your enemies will rise up against you and will be defeated. They will come in one way and flee (*run away or escape*) from you in seven ways. All the people of the earth will be afraid of you.
> The Lord will open the heavens and send rain in their season, and the work of your hand shall always be blessed. You will lend to many nations, but you will borrow from none.
> The Lord shall make you the head and not the tail, for you shall be at the top, never at the bottom.

If you do not hear the voice of the Lord and fail to do all his commandments, statutes, and judgements, you shall be cursed. The Lord will send you back in ships to Egypt and will offer you for sale to your enemies as male and female slaves. And no one will buy you.

I have set before you life and death, blessings and curses. Now choose life so that you and your children may live. If your heart turns away and you worship and serve other gods, the Lord will denounce you, and you will not possess the land I promised, and you will surely perish.

Then Moses spoke these words to the children of Israel. I am one hundred and twenty years old this day. And the Lord said to me, "You cannot go over Jordan." The Lord, your God, will go before you, and Joshua will guide you, as the Lord had said. Be strong and courageous; fear not, for the Lord your God will not leave you nor forsake you, and be not discouraged.

Moses wrote this law in a book from beginning to end and delivered it to the priests, the sons of Levi, and to all the elders of Israel. Then Moses commanded them, "Read this law at the end of every seventh year to all Israelites at the feast of Tabernacles. Gather men, women, children, and strangers to listen carefully and follow the words of the law. Their children who do not know this law must hear and fear the Lord, your God, in the land of Jordan as long as they live."

10. END OF MOSES WORK

After all these, one day the Lord said to Moses, Your days are approaching, and you must die. Call Joshua and present yourselves in the tabernacle of the congregation. Then Moses and Joshua presented themselves. The Lord appeared in a pillar of clouds, and the cloud stood over the entrance of the tent.

And the Lord said to Moses, "You will rest with your fathers. Therefore, now write a song and teach it to the children of Israel. Make them sing the song, which may be a witness for me against them." So Moses wrote the song the same day and taught it to the Israelites.

Then the Lord gave the charge to Joshua and said, "Be strong and courageous, for you will take the Israelites to the land I promised, and I will be with you."

Moses commanded the Levites, who carried the Ark of the Covenant, to place the book of law that he wrote beside the Ark of the Covenant of the Lord. It will be there as a witness against you.

After Moses made an end to speaking all the words of the song to the Israelites, he said, "Set your hearts to all the words that I declare among you this day, that you shall command your children to observe to do. They are not futile words that were told to you, but it is your life that will prolong your days after you cross Jordan and possess it."

On that same day, the Lord told Moses, "Go up to the mountain of Abarim, to mount Nebo, in the land of Moab across from Jericho, and view the land of Canaan that the children of Israel are going to possess. You will die there on the mountain and will join your ancestors, as Aaron, your brother, died on Mount Hor. This is because you broke the faith with me in the presence of the Israelites in the waters of Meribah. Therefore, you will only see the land from a distance, but you will not enter the land that I am going to give the people of Israel."

These are the blessings that Moses, the man of God, blessed the children of Israel before his death.

Reuben: Let Reuben live and not die, and his men will be oversized.

Judah: Lord, hear the voice of Judah. Unite him with his people and deliver him from his enemies.

Levi: Let your Thummim and Urim (*perfections and light*) be with you. Lord, accept the work of his hands and strike down all the people who hate him and rise against him.

Benjamin: He is the beloved of the Lord, and the Lord protects him all day long.

Joseph: Blessed will be his land, with precious things from heaven and the deep waters that lie below. Bless him with precious fruits brought forth by the sun, the finest the moon can yield, and the best gifts of the earth. Let him be blessed for being special compared to his brothers. His glory will be like the firstborn bull, and he will push the people to the ends of the earth with the horn, like the horns of unicorns.

Zebulun: He will rejoice while going out.

Issachar: He will rejoice in his tents.

Zebulun and Issachar shall call the people to the mountain and offer sacrifices of righteousness, and they will feast on the abundance of the seas and the hidden treasures of the sand.

Gad: He will dwell like a lion and will be seated as the lawgiver (*one who provides laws to a society*). He will execute the justice of the Lord and give judgements.

Dan: He is a lion's cub and shall leap from Bashan.

Naphtali: He will be satisfied with the favour of the Lord and will be filled with his blessings. He will possess the West and the South.

Asher: He will be the most blessed of the sons and favoured by his brothers. His shoe soles shall be of iron and brass. His strength will equal his days. The eternal God will be his refuge, and he will drive out his enemies.

Israel shall dwell in safety alone. Jacob will live securely in a land of grain and wine, where the heavens drop dew. Israel, "Happy people you are; who else is like you, the people saved by the Lord? He is your shield and helper. Your enemies shall submit to you, and you shall tread upon (*walk upon*) their high places."

Then Moses went to the mountain of Nebo and climbed to the top of Pisgah. And the Lord showed him the whole land, from Gilead to Dan, the territories of Ephraim and Manasseh, and the land of Judah up to the utmost sea. And the plains of the valley of Jericho, the city of palm trees. And the Lord said to Moses, "This is the land that I promised to Abraham, Isaac, and Jacob. I will give it to your descendants. I have let you see with your eyes, but you will not go there."

And Moses, the servant of the Lord, died there in the land of Moab, according to the word of the Lord. And the Lord buried him in a valley in the land of Moab, but no one knows where his grave is to this day. Moses was one hundred and twenty years old when he died. Yet his eyes were not dim, nor was his strength reduced. The children of Israel grieved the death of Moses on the plains of Moab for thirty days.

Now Joshua was full of spirit and wisdom because Moses had laid his hands upon him. And the children of Israel obeyed him and did just as the Lord had commanded Moses. There never arose a prophet in Israel like Moses, whom the Lord knew face-to-face.

Thank you for being a part of this incredible journey, and we look forward to sharing the next volume 3 with you very soon.

www.ingramcontent.com/pod-product-compliance
Lightning Source LLC
Chambersburg PA
CBHW021221130726
47988CB00002B/766